A FAIRY TALE
— BECOMES A —
Contemporary Classic

By Jessica Ward

becker&mayer!
BOOK PRODUCERS

11120 NE 33rd Place, Suite 101, Bellevue WA, 98004
beckermayer.com

Editor: Leah Jenness
Designer: Megan Sugiyama
Production Coordinators: Cindy Curren and Diane Ross
Art conversion: Kelly Jackson-Browniee

978-1-60380-358-8

This book is part of Disney Frozen Paint-by-Number Kit
and is not to be sold separately.

If you have questions or comments about this product,
please visit www.beckermayer.com/customerservice.html
and click on the customer service request form.

Manufactured in China

BM 14503 - 15240
83450 900 463 0

10 9 8 7 6 5 4 3 2 1

CONTENTS

Paint-by-Number Instructions

To create a *Frozen*-inspired masterpiece, simply match the numbers on
the canvas to the corresponding paints. When you see multiple numbers
listed, mix equal parts of each paint to create new colors. For example, 3/7
is equal parts paint 3 and paint 7, and 5/5/6 is two parts paint 5 and one
part paint 6.

Supplies

- Cup of water for cleaning your brush
- Paper towels for blotting and brush cleaning
- Toothpicks for stirring paint
- Plastic wrap or piece of aluminum foil for paint mixing
- Newspaper or cloth to protect work surface

Tips and Techniques

- Before beginning, refer to the color key for each canvas to see how
  many paint colors are needed and which colors will need to be mixed.
- To open paint pots, press the plastic teeth *toward* one another.
- Stir paint with toothpicks before getting started for best results.
- Smaller areas should be painted first, then move on to larger areas.
- For best results, paint areas that are a single number first, then
  begin color mixing.
- When mixing colors, start by mixing a small amount of paint to
  avoid having paint left over.
- Match mixed paint to the color key given for each canvas before
  applying.
- Let paint dry completely before applying a second coat, if needed.
- Change your brush-cleaning water frequently to keep paint colors
  pure.
- Clean brush with soap and water after use.
- Be sure to close pots completely to avoid the paint drying out when
  not in use.

1　5　2　8　3/10
4　1/4/10　1/10　8/10　9/10
9/10/10　6/9　9　6/8　3/9
4/10　7　4/5　6/7/10　7/10

3/9/5　3/9/5/10　3/9/5/10/10　5/10　5/10/10　10　5　2/3/5/10
6/5/10　6/10　4/5　4/10　6　2/3/10　8　1
4/5/10　6/5/5　7/9　7/9/10　7/9/6　3/9　2/3/5　6/8　1/10
7/9　6/7　10　4　5/10/10　5/10　3　4/6

1　9/2　10　9/10　9/2/10
7/5/10　5/10　7/4/6　7/4　7/4/6/10
6　7　2/4/10　4/10　7/7/4/10
1/10　7/9　9　5

1　5　2　8　3/10
4　1/4/10　1/10　8/10　9/10
9/10/10　6/9　9　6/8　8/10/10
4/5　6/7/10

4/10　1/4　1/4/5　7　7/10　　10　5　4　1　1/10
1/10　1/4/10　4/5　3/9　6/10　　6　3/9/10　3/9　6/10　1/3
6/7/10　5/10　7/9　7/8/10　7/9/6　　7/9　6/7　2/3/13　2　2/3/5/10
5/10/10　5/10　2/4　4/6　2/3/5

PART I.
THE TRANSFORMATION OF A FAIRY TALE

The history of The Walt Disney Company is studded with gems inspired by classic fairy tales. The legacy was cemented with Walt's very first feature-length animated film, *Snow White and the Seven Dwarfs*, which premiered in 1937 to wild success, disproving the doubters who had previously referred to it as "Disney's Folly." Throughout the next few decades, Walt and his animators produced movies and shorts on a variety of subjects, ranging from an Italian

marionette to a flying circus elephant. But from the stories of the Brothers Grimm to the works of Charles Perrault, fairy tales have always inspired The Walt Disney Studios.

Cinderella (1950), *Sleeping Beauty* (1959), *The Little Mermaid* (1989), *Beauty and the Beast* (1991), *The Princess and the Frog* (2009), and *Tangled* (2010) all had their origins in fairy tales, and all became instant classics beloved by generations of viewers. The latest animated addition to this legacy is *Frozen* (2013).

The Snow Queen's New Role

The story of *Frozen* is loosely based on Hans Christian Andersen's fairy tale "The Snow Queen," first published in 1844.

Andersen's story tells of two children—a girl named Gerda and a boy named Kai—who are neighbors and best friends. But when tiny shards of an enchanted evil mirror get into one of Kai's eyes and into his heart, he becomes cruel and sees ugliness in everything . . . everything except snowflakes. That winter, when Kai is out playing in the snow, the Snow Queen appears, kisses him to make him forget Gerda, and takes him away to her palace. The townspeople believe Kai drowned in a nearby river, but Gerda refuses to give

up searching for him. Gerda's pure and innocent heart leads her through many trials, and with the help of a few friends and a reindeer, she eventually reaches the Snow Queen's palace. When she finds Kai, blue and nearly frozen solid, he does not remember her. Gerda weeps over him, and her warm tears thaw his flesh and dissolve the shards of icy mirror lodged in his heart. His memories return to him, and he and Gerda travel home together.

Walt Disney actually began development on an animated version of "The Snow Queen" shortly after the release of *Snow White and the Seven Dwarfs*. Chris Buck, director of *Frozen*, comments, "I think that Walt was attracted to the Hans Christian Andersen stories because he's the same kind of storyteller. Walt would tell very rich, very deep, sometimes dark stories, but also had the whimsy and the humor, and it would take you to another world. It was in 1939 that Walt had given 'The Snow Queen' [along with other Hans Christian Andersen stories] a production number." Buck's fellow director, Jennifer Lee, who was also the screenwriter for *Frozen*, adds, "There were talks about doing a biography of Hans Christian Andersen, working with MGM to do the live-action and Disney would do the animation. But we don't know what happened to that. So there's this huge mystery, wondering what drew [Walt] to 'The Snow Queen' and what he was hoping to do."

Animation historians speculate that "The Snow Queen" was perhaps intended to be one of the animated sequences in the shelved Hans Christian Andersen project, but no evidence has been found to show that creative work ever began on such a segment. "The Ugly Duckling"—one of Andersen's short stories—was made into two Silly Symphony cartoons released in 1931 and 1939, and some preliminary development work was done on "The Little Mermaid," although it was ultimately shelved for nearly forty years.

When the filmmakers decided to put "The Snow Queen" back into the production pipeline, they were faced with some adaptation challenges. Lee recounts, "Hans Christian Andersen's story 'The Snow Queen' is very poetic, it's very symbolic, it's episodic, and I think that was the greatest challenge of trying to crack the story." Buck continues, "We took the original theme from the original 'Snow Queen,' and that was 'love conquers negativity.' And for us, the negativity for today is fear. So we took basic things, combined characters, and tried to somewhat simplify the story—and we added a lot of humor to it also."

Inspired by the titular character of Andersen's fairytale, Elsa was originally intended to be the villain of the story, with Anna as the Gerda-like protagonist. But as work on the film progressed—and especially after the filmmakers decided to make Anna and Elsa sisters, and songwriters Robert Lopez and Kristen Anderson-Lopez wrote "Let It Go"—it became clear to the production team that Elsa was not evil; she was merely misunderstood. The plot was rewritten into a love story—not one about a boy and a girl, but one about family.

The Fairy Tale Becomes a Musical

Music has been an integral part of Disney animation since the very beginning. Before the release of *The Jazz Singer* in 1927, all films were silent, and the projections were accompanied by live pianists or organists who played in the theater. Always the pioneer, Walt felt that a synchronized sound cartoon was the next monumental advance in animation, and in 1928, he produced a short called *Steamboat Willie* that included a recorded soundtrack. However, many distributors believed that synchronized sound was just a passing fad, and so would not agree to buy the short. Walt refused to give up; he used his own money to sponsor a two-week screening of

Steamboat Willie—which starred a brand-new character called Mickey Mouse. The rest is movie history.

Many Disney films since *Steamboat Willie* have featured memorable music and songs, and a number of those pieces have won Academy Awards® and Grammy Awards®. "When You Wish Upon a Star" from *Pinocchio* (1940), "Chim Chim Cher-ee" from *Mary Poppins* (1964), "Under the Sea" from *The Little Mermaid* (1989), and "You'll Be in My Heart" from *Tarzan* (1999) are just a few of the Disney compositions that have won the Academy Award for Best Song. These melodies are inextricable parts of the fabric of the movies for which they were written, and yet they have also become stand-alone successes, earning popularity beyond the context of their films.

When it came time to choose songwriters for *Frozen*, the filmmakers knew that they needed talented musicians who could help tell the story through song. Having created the off-beat popular musical *Avenue Q* with collaborator Jeff Marx, and then going on to compose the music for Broadway smash *The Book of Mormon* with Trey Parker and Matt Stone, Robert Lopez was already well known and highly praised. He and his wife, Kristen Anderson-Lopez, cowrote several songs for the 2011

Disney film *Winnie the Pooh*, and they were a natural choice for the *Frozen* team.

The couple's involvement with the film began very early in development. Anderson-Lopez recalls, "Every single day for eighteen months we had a conference call from twelve to two with the filmmakers Jennifer Lee and Chris Buck. And we would just talk about, 'Who was Anna; what does she want? Who was Elsa; why does she do what she does? Who do they need to interact with for their journeys to happen?' . . . We would attack different moments in the film like a problem we had to solve. And sometimes they would

be solved by [saying] 'Let's do this musically.' Sometimes it would be 'Oh no, this feels like dialogue. Let's do that dialogue.' But it was a whole; the arc of the story was first."

Elaborating on their songwriting process, Lopez says he and Anderson-Lopez had conversation after conversation "about what the characters wanted and how they would get from point A to point B, because the songs need to serve the story. If the songs don't do any storytelling work, then they don't belong in a film like this. So it was us talking and talking, getting ideas for rhymes, getting inspiration for the music of the song, and then by the end of a day or two . . . usually we had all the raw material we'd need to write it. And then it would usually go pretty quickly after that."

Originally, Elsa was a villain and had no relation to Anna. She was fated to create and command an army of snowmen who would wreak havoc on the kingdom. The composition of Elsa's transformation song, "Let It Go," proved to be the second of two tremendous shifts in the film's trajectory. The first came during a brainstorming session, when someone on the film team wondered aloud, "What if Anna and Elsa were sisters?" The idea that the two girls were family added a fascinating angle to the story the filmmakers wanted to tell, and gave depth to Elsa's character.

The second major shift came after this, when Lopez and Anderson-Lopez wrote Elsa's song. "Sometimes Elsa did villainous things and sometimes she was the protagonist, but with 'Let It Go' . . . once you have a character who sings with this amount of

emotion, she couldn't be the villain anymore," Anderson-Lopez
recalls. The song helped humanize Elsa and made viewers
sympathize with her fears. "We put ourselves in the mind-set of
someone who'd leave everything behind and be stuck out on a
mountain, and how cold and scared she would be at that moment,"
Anderson-Lopez says. Lopez adds, "We sent the demo out and
everyone went 'Oh, my gosh, that's great.'"

Idina Menzel, who provided Elsa's voice, affirms that sentiment.
"The first time I heard 'Let It Go' I thought, 'Wow, this isn't just the
funny sort of evil queen song.' It was a real, soulful, emotional,
vulnerable song. And then, to my beautiful surprise, she was never,
ever the nemesis, really. She's just the misunderstood young
woman that we can all relate to."

Less than six months after the film's soundtrack was released, the album had held the top spot on the Billboard 200 list for thirteen nonconsecutive weeks, selling more than 2.6 million copies. And at the 2014 Academy Awards, "Let It Go" won the Oscar for Best Song, placing Robert Lopez and Kristen Anderson-Lopez in the ranks of the legendary composers and musicians who have contributed to the canon of award-winning Disney songs, including Robert and Richard Sherman, Alan Menken, Howard Ashman, Tim Rice, Elton John, and Phil Collins.

Giving Voice to the Fairy Tale

Finding the right actors to voice the characters in his films was a high priority for Walt Disney. He himself was the voice of Mickey Mouse for years, giving it up only when the demands of being a studio head proved to be too numerous. Walt had a keen eye for talent, hiring novices and veterans alike. Once he identified a gifted voice actor, he would often recruit that person for multiple films. For example, actress Verna Felton played the Fairy Godmother in *Cinderella*, the Queen of Hearts in *Alice in Wonderland* (1951), and Aunt Sarah in *Lady and the Tramp* (1955), among other roles.

The *Frozen* filmmakers auditioned hundreds of actors and actresses in their search to find the right voices for Elsa, Anna, Hans, Kristoff, and Olaf.

Having built most of her résumé underneath the bright lights of Broadway, Menzel, who played Maureen in *Rent* and then Elphaba in *Wicked*—for which she won a Tony Award®—brought a unique sensibility to the role of Elsa. She identified with Elsa's struggle to embrace her power, recalling her own growing pains. "I felt that way when I was a kid," she says. "I had this voice, and I didn't want to show it off at school and I didn't want to seem like I was conceited or bragging, so I would hide it all the time . . . I completely related to this character."

But it wasn't just her powerful singing voice that made Menzel perfect for the role. Buck recalls, "Idina Menzel, besides being a fantastic Broadway actress and singer . . . she's so perfect for this part because she has this vulnerability in her voice. Even though she plays a very strong character, and Idina's a very strong woman herself, it's so perfect for Elsa because Elsa is a very vulnerable character."

An experienced actress best known for her roles in the television series *Veronica Mars* and the film *Forgetting Sarah Marshall*, Kristen Bell

was chosen for the part of Anna, the younger princess of Arendelle. Of the casting process, Buck recalls, "Kristen was the first person to audition for the role of Anna. We did audition hundreds of other actresses, but Kristen was always the bar and no one could quite get there." Kristen took the role, and "we . . . couldn't be happier," Buck says. "I think Kristen has become Anna, or Anna has become Kristen. I don't know which one it is, but she brought so much to this part. She brought her humor; she brought her charm, her spontaneity. She did great improvisation for us."

Menzel could not be more complimentary of her costar. "It's been so much fun working with Kristen. I'm a huge fan of hers. Often when you're recording these things you're not always in the same room with [your costars], but we've had an opportunity to

really work off of each other in person and we just found a lot of great nuances and spontaneous moments, improvised a little bit. She's such a great actress, and I think she does a beautiful job with this character. She's really funny and idiosyncratic and lovable."

For Kristoff, the ice-selling mountain man who reluctantly guides Anna on her quest, the filmmakers cast Jonathan Groff, who has starred in several television series, including *Glee*, *Boss*, and *Looking*, and is a Broadway star as well ("Spring Awakening"). Of his experience playing the reclusive reindeer fan, Groff says, "Probably my favorite thing about him is he's not your typical Disney leading man. He's got a stockier body, which I can relate

to, and he's scrappy. He's got a sense of humor, and I think he's the perfect foil for the character of Anna . . . because Anna is not your typical Disney leading lady, either. She's got a sense of humor, and they both actually grew up sort of alone and Kristoff has lived in the woods by himself for a long time. His only companion is his reindeer, Sven . . . You see in the movie, he does a sort of voice for Sven's thoughts, which is also one of my favorite elements of Kristoff."

Prince Hans, the ultimate villain of the story, is played by Santino Fontana, who has acted in Broadway's *Billy Elliot*, *The Importance of Being Earnest*, and *Cinderella*. In spite of his character's devious actions, Fontana really enjoyed giving Hans his voice. "Hans is a prince; he is a Disney prince, but he is more than a Disney prince. He's many things, and there are a lot of secrets and twists and turns that we take with Hans. And you won't see them coming, which is great—and a great thing to play, an awesome character to play. Because he's not what he seems at first. But no one really is."

Much of the comedy in *Frozen* is embodied in the person—er, *snowperson* of Olaf, a snowman magically created by Elsa based on one she and Anna made as kids. The voice of Olaf is provided by Josh Gad, who played Elder Arnold Cunningham in *The Book of Mormon* and has also appeared on numerous television shows including *Back to You*, *Modern Family*, and *New Girl*. In addition to relishing the opportunities for humor that the role afforded, Gad appreciated the symbolism of Olaf. "He's still trapped in that childhood purity |and| innocence of what they were as girls, and that's what is so beautiful … that he connects them to their past, when the future was full of optimism and the sky was the limit," Gad says.

Animating a Frozen Fairy Tale

When it came to the technology of animation, Walt Disney was
constantly experimenting, inventing, and setting the standard
within the filmmaking industry. He and his fellow creative
wizards pioneered the use of the multiplane camera, which
allowed up to seven tiers of artwork to be shot at once, creating
the illusion of depth in a two-dimensional world. Walt was also
in the habit of sending his animators on research trips, the most
famous of which being their goodwill tour of South America,
which led to the production of *Saludos Amigos* (1943) and *The Three
Caballeros* (1945).

Walt's innovative spirit and commitment to detail are still alive today, and the *Frozen* filmmakers were keen to do thorough research for the film. They began by traveling to the land that birthed Hans Christian Andersen and his fairy tales: Scandinavia. "We did draw a lot of inspiration from Norway," says producer Peter Del Vecho. "In fact, we sent our art direction team to Norway as the jumping-off point." Buck praises the value of the trip, adding, "Norway was so inspirational to us and our team. Everything in the movie—the costumes, the architecture—came from that trip."

When it came to creating the individual characters, the animators looked to the voice actors, much like Walt's animators employed footage of live-action reference models performing scenes in costume. Of her time spent in the sound booth, Bell recalls, "You're always recorded. So you can come to work in your pajamas, but someone is going to view that tape. So, you have two cameras on you at all times to catch itsy-bitsy, imperceptible movements of your face, of your eyebrows, where you use your hands. It adds so much dimension to these characters."

Becky Bresee, animation supervisor for Anna, could not agree more. "I did look at Kristen's recording sessions, and what I got from [them] was just some of the goofy, real-girl things she'd do, just by watching her expressions." She continues, "Kristen brought this wonderful, goofy, real-girl character that people can relate to because she has her faults, and everybody does, so it really makes the character come to life and become believable."

In addition to Bell's tapes, Bresee had a few other sources of inspiration: herself and her daughters. The mother of two young girls, Bresee filmed her children acting out the scene when Anna jumps on Elsa's bed to wake her up in the morning. And when she needed reference footage for adult Anna, she filmed herself. "I have a camera at my desk," she relates, "and I shoot a little movie of myself acting the scene out. That's part of the joy of my job."

Wayne Unten, animation supervisor for Elsa, viewed Menzel's reference footage, and he also spoke to her about the anatomy of singing. "She talked about how, when singing, you use your diaphragm," he says. "It's very subtle." Unten created a control in his computer animation program that would simulate the expansion and compression of Elsa's diaphragm when she sings. "You can kind of get the sense that she's actually breathing," he says. "It's a puppet—it's not real—but you want to make sure that it feels like she's taking in oxygen and she's breathing."

Animator Hyrum Osmond served as animation supervisor for Olaf. "Olaf is an animator's dream," Osmond enthuses. "Here's a character that you can pull apart, put back together in different

forms; there's a lot you can do with him." Like Bresee and Unten, Osmond looked to the voice actor's session tapes for source material. "Olaf's not Olaf without Josh Gad. Josh would go into that recording booth and just put himself into it. Just the little movements and especially his facial expressions were very helpful."

Capturing the nuances of the voice actors' facial expressions wasn't solely important for the sake of making the characters look real; it was integral to communicating the feeling of the film. Chief creative officer of the Walt Disney Animation Studios John Lasseter maintains the importance of animating lifelike characters: "The directors and myself, we talked to the animators in terms of emotion. It's like you look at those faces and that character is alive."

PART II.

A NINETEENTH-CENTURY FAIRY TALE WITH A TWENTY-FIRST-CENTURY TWIST

With regard to its fairy tale origin story, music, voice actors, and character animat ion, *Frozen* is a quintessential Disney film. And like every Disney film, this one puts its own unique and sincere take on classic themes and motifs found throughout literature, film, and other media. *Frozen* also uses tried-and-true traditional storytelling, but with today's audiences in mind—

just one of the reasons it is so appealing for boys and girls, young and old alike.

A glance at the American Film Institute's list of the 100 Greatest American Films of All Time shows that a theme common among many selections—from *Gone with the Wind* to *West Side Story*, from *The Sound of Music* to *Titanic*—is love. The same commonality can be found in most Disney animated films, especially those based on fairy tales: *Snow White and the Seven Dwarfs*, *Cinderella*, *Sleeping Beauty*, and *The Little Mermaid* all involve love stories in their larger tales about adventure and destiny. But *Frozen* is different. While it does possess a side plot involving romantic love, the main focus of the movie is familial love, and, more specifically, sisterly love.

There are certainly some Disney animated films that have explored this familial feeling. *Dumbo* (1941) and *Bambi* (1942) both paid homage to the mother figure. *Tarzan* followed the path of a young man striving to find acceptance in family that was not his own, *Lilo & Stitch* (2002) addressed the notion of *'ohana* in a family that had experienced loss but also gained an unconventional member, and *Brother Bear* (2003) delved into the relationship of three brothers who struggle to find their place—with each other and within their community. But when it comes to sisters, Disney animated films had, for the most part, not explored that extraordinary bond very deeply.

Sure, sisters are featured in Disney films. There's Lilo and Nani; Cinderella and her stepsisters, Anastasia and Drizella; and Ariel is the youngest of Triton's seven daughters. However, these characters have adventures that take them beyond their immediate family, and they often have to face their challenges alone or with friends by their side.

From the very first scene of *Frozen* when Anna sings, "Do You Want to Build a Snowman?" it's clear that the story is going to be about a different kind of love, one that's tender yet strong, playful yet unconditional: the love of sisters. "This film is a lot more about the love of family than it is about romantic love," says Bell. "It's kind of a sharp left turn for Disney because of that. No one is waiting for their Prince Charming in this movie, and it's really about whatever you identify as your family or your support system; it's about loving those people ferociously. And especially the love of siblings—how you can fight with them, and you can love them, and you can fight with them again, but if anyone [else] tries to fight with your sibling, good luck [to them] because now you're in defense mode [to protect your sibling]."

Identifying with her character was easy for Bell. "I adored my sisters when I was growing up, but I could definitely relate to

wanting to be closer to them than they wanted to be to me when I was the little runt." She continues, "There's a built-in hierarchy when you have siblings, and the older ones are always cool. The younger ones just so badly want approval. It's a pretty monumental moment when your older sister—I know this because I have two older sisters—gives you an adult compliment."

Menzel also had no difficulty in finding a touchstone for her role. "I have a younger sister. She's three years younger than me. Her name is Cara. We're super close. I'm so super protective of her like an older sister. I used to get up in people's faces if anybody

was mean to my sister. I would compromise or hide any secret if it meant saving my sister in some way."

The parents of two young girls, Lopez and Anderson-Lopez did not have to look far for inspiration when writing songs for Anna and Elsa. Anderson-Lopez comments, "We see this dynamic . . . on a much smaller scale. But to have the older daughter slam the door and the younger daughter to be like 'Please won't you play dolls with me?' . . . that kind of inspired the 'Do You Want to Build a Snowman?' song."

The theme of sibling love resonates with Gad as well. "I'm a father," he relates, "so for me, this movie couldn't speak more to that experience. And what I love is, you talk about the idea of family, but it's really the idea of siblings and how strong that bond is. And as somebody who grew up with two brothers, I think I would melt for them. I think that I would make that sacrifice . . . that bond is what connects you when you're at rock bottom, when you're at your happiest and you need someone to share it with. You share the same DNA, but not just in the scientific sense, but in the sense of your past, your history. Nobody knows you better. Nobody knows your weaknesses and your strengths better than them, even when they take advantage of those weaknesses and beat up on you."

Groff feels similarly about the importance of the film's message. "I think that more than any other Disney movie, *Frozen* sort of redefines what true love is . . . in a really surprising and beautiful way. And I think that that is really a great message to be sending to the kids that are going to see this movie because Disney movies, I think inevitably, are a part of our makeup growing up and so to have a message that is about love and about family is really important, and certainly that means a lot to me."

It speaks volumes of the tropes to which audiences are accustomed that up until the very end of the film, the viewers—and the characters themselves—expect Anna's frozen heart to be thawed by an act of true love performed by one of her romantic interests. The true departure and defining moment of *Frozen* happens when Anna, nearly inert due to the ice overtaking her body, puts herself between Hans's sword and the cowering Elsa. It is Anna's own sacrifice—the unwavering love that she feels for her sister—that thaws Anna's heart and allows Elsa to unfreeze the kingdom.

A Folk Tale for Modern Folks

While the theme of sisterly love certainly sets *Frozen* apart in the company of its fellow Disney films, it's the realization of the characters that makes the film a stand-alone success. These

characters are three-dimensional, they're real—characters who wake up with drool dribbling out of their mouths, who readily admit to eating their own boogers, and who make jokes about the dangers of yellow snow. These princesses aren't immune to the mundane afflictions of frizzy hair, food cravings, and uncontrollable burps.

The *Frozen* filmmakers put concerted effort into making Anna, Elsa, Kristoff, Hans, and Olaf relatable, imperfect, tangible characters, aided in their efforts by the voice actors, who wholeheartedly embraced those intentions. "Voicing a Disney heroine has been a dream of mine for a very long time," Bell affirms. She wanted people watching the film to recognize themselves in Anna. To achieve that, she thought about herself growing up. "I didn't hold my hands just so, and I put my foot in my mouth a lot. I talk too fast and too much and too much to myself, and I wanted to create a character that little kids who felt, kind of, weirder than most could relate to."

Bell continues, "I kept pushing for her to be quirkier and goofier because that's how I felt as a kid growing up. I sort of embraced having a not-so-standard princess personality. I really wanted to make Anna just different, and I wanted her to be a role model for little girls who are like me." Many of the growing pains and personal

struggles that might have plagued Disney princesses of the past were largely kept off the screen, whereas with Anna, viewers actually witness her waking up with hair in her mouth, see her gorging on chocolate, and hear her admitting that she's awkward.

Gad, who improvised many of his scenes as Olaf, loved the idea of making the characters as believable as possible. "I also think that the characteristics and the actors that they've chosen to portray these characters have brought such an interesting nuance," he says. "Let me speak to Kristen Bell's character of Anna. It's a princess unlike any other I've ever seen before. Warts and all, she's a neurotic, bumbling mess, and I love that. I love that I've never seen that character before. I've never seen that kind of bubbly little character that I think is so unique and fresh. And Elsa is her own kind of breed of this powerful woman who is trying to control what she's capable of, but again, it's done in a way that I think is refreshing and very different . . . And I think that the reason that people are reacting so positively to this is that we're telling stories that are as old as time, but they're being told with a very unique approach to them that's almost very modern and it has a very of-the-now sensibility to it."

Giving the film's characters more rounded and human personalities did not make them any less aspirational or detract

from their appeal in any way—in fact, it did just the opposite. It imparts a message of self-love, of embracing all of a person's qualities—both the positives and the negatives—because those all combine in a recipe that makes each person who they are. Bell puts it succinctly when she says, "It's this overarching idea of loving your flaws. Maybe you're clumsy and maybe that's wonderful because that makes you unique and it makes you different."

AFTERWORD

How is the success of a film measured? It could be by the number of tickets sold at the box office, or by how many people dress up as characters from the movie the following Halloween. Perhaps it's the percentage of children who list items of film-related merchandise like dolls or DVDs on their Christmas lists.

But maybe the real measure of a film's influence is how deeply it affects culture—how often it's brought up in person-to-person interaction, appears on social media, or inspires other forms of artistic expression.

By any standards, Frozen has surely ascended the ranks of cinema's pantheon. During 2014, it became the fifth-highest-grossing film in history, and the number one animated film of all time.

But that's just the tip of the iceberg (pun intended). Frozen has taken the world by (ice) storm. Its soundtrack is hugely popular. "Let

It Go" is a smash hit that's played everywhere from school dances to weddings. Idina Menzel has appeared on several television shows to perform the song, including a popular rendition with the Roots on *The Tonight Show Starring Jimmy Fallon*. The world created for the film

has found its way into real life, as well. Audiences want to look like the characters—to take a walk in their "snowshoes." For example, Anna's and Elsa's trademark hair styles have become hugely popular. The story has touched audiences that deeply.

Anna and Elsa's story continues on in different forms. Other incarnations of the tale include a stage adaptation, as well as an animated short that the original filmmaking team, including Jennifer Lee and Chris Buck, created, called *Frozen Fever*.

The story continues, and is so beloved and so successful, because at its heart *Frozen* is a tale told with love, humor, and warmth that manages to defy expectations while reflecting reality at the same time. It's a movie that redefines the meaning of true love. And that can thaw any frozen heart.